Note to Parents and Teachers

The READING ABOUT: STARTERS series introduces key science vocabulary to young children while encouraging them to discover and understand the world around them. The series works as a set of graded readers in three levels.

LEVEL 2: BEGIN TO READ ALONE follows guidelines set out in the National Curriculum for Year 2 in schools. These books can be read alone or as part of guided or group reading. Each book has three sections:

• Information pages that introduce key words. These key words appear in bold for easy recognition on pages where the related science concepts are explained.
• A lively story that recalls this vocabulary and encourages children to use these words when they talk and write.
• A quiz and index ask children to look back and recall what they have read.

Questions for Further Investigation

WHAT FLOATS? explains key concepts about FLOATING and SINKING. Here are suggestions for further discussion linked to the questions on the information spreads:

p. 5 *Does your body float or sink?* It can do both! If you stretch your body flat, you can float. But if you curl up into a ball, your body will sink.

p. 7 *What heavy objects have you seen floating?* e.g. boats and ships, heavy logs or tree trunks, animals such as swans or crocodiles. Ask children to think about why they float.

p. 9 *Why are icebergs dangerous to ships at sea?* Ships sometimes bump into icebergs floating in the sea. The hard ice can make a hole in a ship, causing it to sink.

p. 11 *Why do you think a raft floats well?* A flat shape like a raft floats well because the weight is spread out. A flat piece of silver foil floats. But if you roll it into a ball, it sinks!

p. 13 *Do you think things float better in deep water?* If you put a plastic boat in a swimming pool it would float just as well in the shallow end as in the deep end.

p. 15 *What happens to the water level when you get in a bath?* The water level gets higher, because your body has taken up some of the space where the water was before you got in.

p. 17 *What uses air to h* **700031452535** , and hovercraft.

p. 19 *Can air inside you* helps your body float.

p. 23 *What animals ca* sh, jellyfish, frogs, some snakes, crocodiles, turtles, insects such as water beetles, birds such as ducks and swans, dolphins, whales, hippopotamuses, seals, bears, dogs, tigers and humans!

ADVISORY TEAM

Educational Consultant
Andrea Bright – Science Co-ordinator, Trafalgar Junior School, Twickenham

Literacy Consultant
Jackie Holderness – former Senior Lecturer in Primary Education, Westminster Institute, Oxford Brookes University

Series Consultants
Anne Fussell – Early Years Teacher and University Tutor, Westminster Institute, Oxford Brookes University

David Fussell – C.Chem., FRSC

D1100730

CONTENTS

© Aladdin Books Ltd 2006

Designed and produced by
Aladdin Books Ltd
2/3 Fitzroy Mews
London W1T 6DF

First published in 2006

ISBN 978 07496 6846 4 (H'bk)
ISBN 978 07496 7027 6 (P'bk)

A catalogue record for this
book is available from the
British Library.
Dewey Classification: 532'.02

l in Malaysia
its reserved

Sally Hewitt
er: Jim Pipe
Design: Flick, Book
& Graphics

to: The pupils of Trafalgar
School, Twickenham, for
ng as models in this book.

Photocredits:
*l-left, r-right, b-bottom, t-top,
c-centre, m-middle*
Cover tl & b, 4 both, 8, 9t, 10t,
12b, 13, 14 both, 24 both, 25t,
27t, 28-29 all, 31tr, ml, mr & bl
— istockphoto.com. Cover tc, 2bl,
3, 9b, 11t, 18, 20 both, 22br, 25b,
27b, 30t, 31bc, 32 — Photodisc.
Cover tl, 12t, 26b — Comstock.
2tl, 23tr — TongRo. 2ml, 5, 10b,
23b — Corbis. 6-7 all, 11b, 15, 17
both, 19t — Marc Arundale /
Select Pictures. 16tl, 21 — US
Navy. 16b — Digital Vision. 19,
31br — Stockbyte. 22t — Select
Pictures. 26t — Ingram Publishing.

FLOATING
AND SINKING

What Floats?

By Jim Pipe

Aladdin/Watts
London • Sydney

A *floating leaf*

Do you know what
floats or **sinks**?

A log **floats** on **water**.
A leaf **floats**
across a pond.

But when you drop a
small stone into the **water**, it **sinks**!

4

Boat

Look at this picture of the sea.
The **boat floats** on the **water**.

When something **floats**,
it sits on top of the **water**.
When it **sinks**, it drops to the bottom.

• Does your body float or sink?

This girl is testing what sinks and floats.

She collects some objects: an orange, a fork, a glass marble, a block of wood, a stone, a cork and a plastic cup.

This boy holds the objects in his hands.

Some feel **heavy**, some feel **light**.

He guesses what will float and what will sink.

They put the objects into a bowl of water.

They make a chart and write down what floats and what sinks.

Even if just part of an object is above the surface, it is still floating.

Are you surprised that an orange floats?

Heavy things sometimes float. Think of a big ship.

	Floats	Sinks
Glass		✓
Wood	✓	
Plastic	✓	
Metal		✓
Orange	✓	

• What heavy objects have you seen floating?

Some **materials** float better than others.

A **wooden** spoon floats.
So does a plastic spoon.
But a metal spoon does not float.

Things made from **wood** float well.
In the past, ships were made from **wood**.

Wooden ship

Iceberg

Ice floats. An iceberg is a big lump of **ice** floating in the sea. Most of the iceberg is below the water.

Oil also floats on water. When oil spills from a ship, it floats. It may wash onto a beach.

• Why are icebergs dangerous to ships at sea?

The **shape** of an object can help it float. That's why a boat has a special **shape**.

If you **stretch** out in the water, you float. But if you curl up in a ball, you sink!

Boat shape

The part of a boat that sits in the water is its hull.

Some boats have two or three hulls.

A ball of clay sinks in water. But if you change the clay's **shape**, it floats.

This boy rolls out the clay. He **stretches** it into a boat **shape**.

When he puts the clay boat in the water, it floats!

• Why do you think a raft floats well?

A small metal ball sinks,
but a big metal ship floats.
Why is this?

Tennis ball

Here's one way to find
out. **Push** a tennis ball
under the water.

The water seems to
push the ball up again!

Now **push** a football under the water.
The water **pushes** back even harder.

That's because the football takes up
more **space** in the water.

Football

A boat shape takes up lots of
space in the water, so the water
gives it a big **push** upwards.
This helps a ship float.

• Do you think things float better in deep water?

A boat's shape helps it carry a heavy load.

This ship carries heavy containers. They make it float **lower** in the water.

When the ship has unloaded the containers, it floats **higher** in water.

Big cranes load containers onto a ship.

14

This boy is testing a plastic tub to see how much it can carry.

He fills the tub with blocks, one at a time. The tub gets **lower** and **lower** in the water.

When he takes blocks out of the tub, it floats **higher** in the water.

• What happens to the water level when you get in a bath?

What happens to a boat if it gets **full** of water?

The boat gets too heavy and it sinks.

In a storm, big waves can fill a ship with water and make it sink.

This rescue boat stays afloat even if a big wave knocks it over.

A sinking ship

You can see how water
makes an object sink.

Look at these three bottles.
One is **full** of water.
One is half **full**.
One is **empty**.

The **empty** bottle floats high in the water.
The half **full** bottle floats low in the water.
But the **full** bottle sinks!

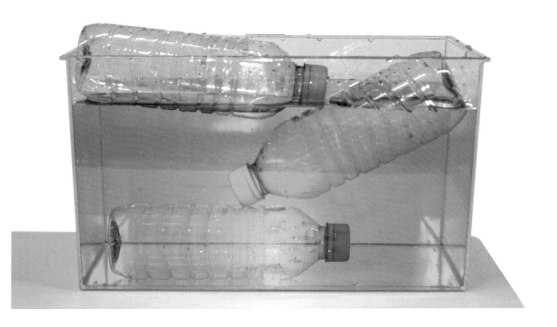

• What uses air to help it float?

The **air** inside an object helps it to float.

The hull of a canoe is shaped so that there is lots of **air** inside.
This **air** helps a canoe float.

Canoe

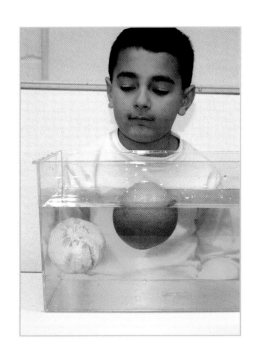

If you put an orange in water, it floats. If you peel it, then put it in water, it sinks!

The peel **traps air** inside the orange. The **air** helps it float.

Feathers also trap air.
This air helps a duck float.

• Can air inside you help you float?

This boat is full of air. You pump air into the sides. You **inflate** it.

You **blow** air into a rubber ring. You **inflate** it. The air in the ring helps you to float.

20

Submarine

A submarine can float and sink.
Inside its hull are big tanks.

When water fills the tanks, the
submarine sinks. When air fills the tanks,
the submarine floats to the surface.

• Would a rubber ring help you float if there
was no air inside it?

There are different reasons why things float. Can you remember them?

Materials like wood float well.

Shapes that take up lots of space in the water float well.

Air helps objects to float. Think of a beach ball.

Salt water also helps things to float.

The **sea** is very **salty**, so things float better in the **sea** than in a swimming pool.

A shark does not float. It swims.
When it stops swimming, it sinks!

• What animals can swim?

SINK OR SWIM?

*Look out for words about **floating** and **sinking**.*

My big brother Greg and sister Kate love going to the beach.

They swim in the **sea**. They go for a ride in a **boat**.

I don't like swimming.
I can't **float** like my sister.
I am afraid I will **sink**
like a stone.

I play on the
beach instead.

"Would you like to swim, too?" asks Mum.

"No thanks," I say.

The **water** is too cold.

The waves splash me.

The **sea** tastes **salty**. It makes my eyes sting.

"That's OK," says Dad.
"We can go to the
pool tomorrow.
The **water** is warm.
The pool is shallow."

The pool is not
deep like the **sea**.
But I am worried.

There might be
fish in the pool.
They will bite me!

Dad gives me some goggles.
Slowly I put my face in the **water**.
I open my eyes. I can see!
There are no fish. Just Kate smiling at me!

"Try to **float**," says Mum. "I'll hold onto you."
"I will **sink**," I say.
"Hold onto Mum," says Dad.

"**Stretch** out," says Mum.
I make a long **shape**
in the **water**, like
the hull of a **boat**.

We go to the pool every day.
Soon I can **float**.
But I don't want to let go of Mum.

One day, Dad drops his flip flops into the pool. "Look how they **float**," he says.

"This board is also made from a **light material**. It will help you **float!**"

I **push** hard on the board, but it does not **sink!**

I hang on to the board. I kick my legs.

I can swim!

Soon we are having lots of fun in the pool.
Dad **blows air** into a big **inflatable** ring.

When it is **full** of **air**, Dad sits on the ring.
It gets **lower** and **lower** in the water.

We all shout, "You're too **heavy!**"

Mum blows **air** into a small **inflatable** ring.
It helps me **float**.

Now I love swimming.

Next year I will
swim in the **sea**.
Kate says it is easy to
float in **salt water**.

One day I want to be a diver and swim
under the **water**. I will swim like a fish!

Think about your day. What things around
you **float** or **sink**? Write them down in a
list. Or draw a picture of machines or
animals that **float** or **sink**.

A submarine sinks
under the water.

A fishing boat floats
on the sea.

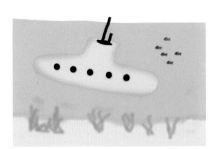

QUIZ

What **material** were
old ships made of?

Answer on page 8

How can you help
your body **float**?

Answer on page 10

What happens to a
ship when it carries
a **heavy** load?

Answer on page 14

What helps these
objects to float?

Have you read this book? Well done! Do you remember these words? Look back and find out.

INDEX